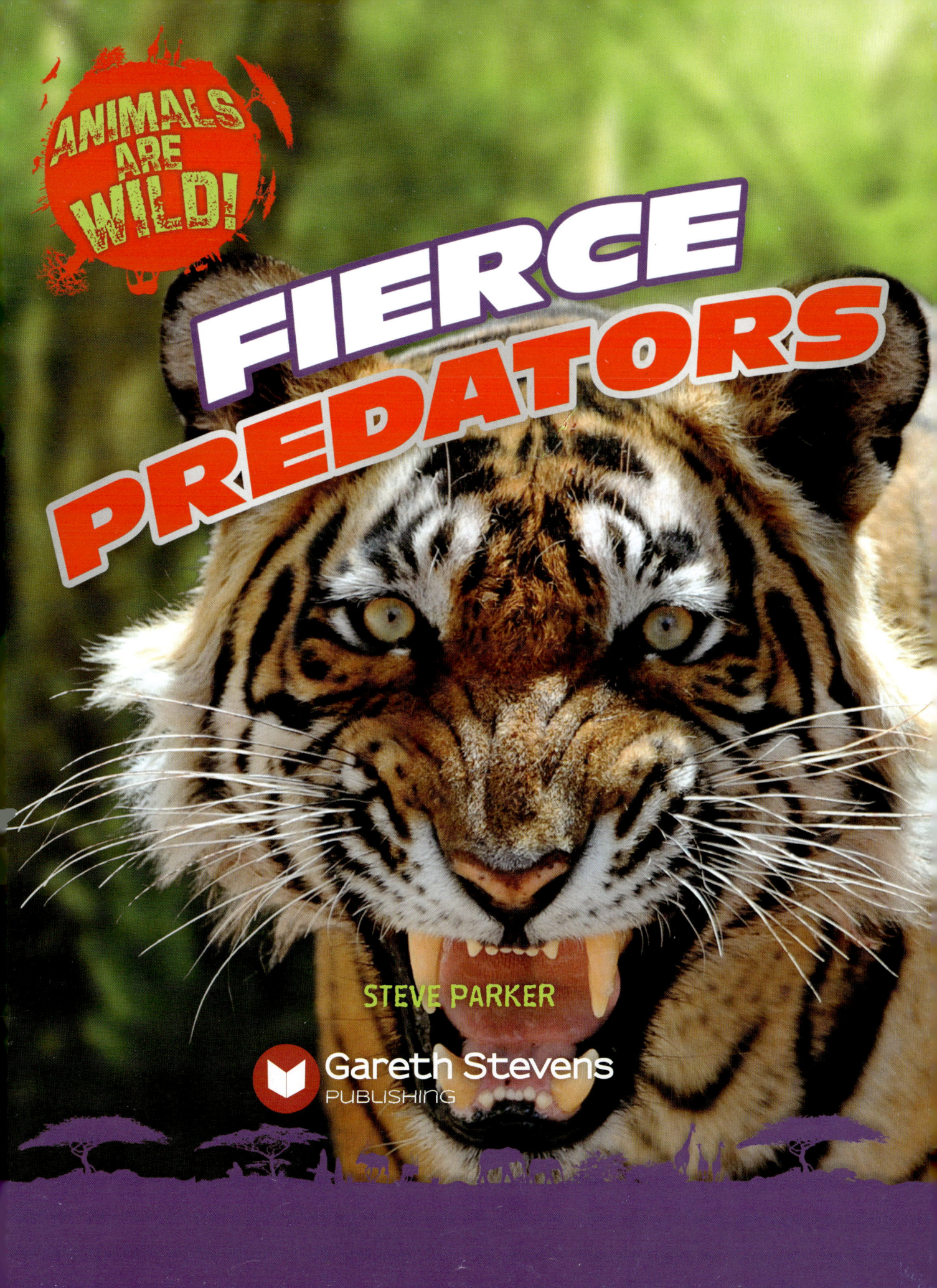

ANIMALS ARE WILD!

FIERCE PREDATORS

STEVE PARKER

Gareth Stevens
PUBLISHING

Please visit our website, www.garethstevens.com.
For a free color catalog of all our high-quality books, call toll free 1-800-542-2595 or fax 1-877-542-2596

Cataloging-in-Publication Data

Names: Parker, Steve.
Title: Fierce predators / Steve Parker.
Description: New York : Gareth Stevens Publishing, 2016. | Series: Animals are wild! | Includes index.
Identifiers: ISBN 9781482450064 (pbk.) | ISBN 9781482450088 (library bound) | ISBN 9781482450071 (6 pack)
Subjects: LCSH: Predatory animals--Juvenile literature.
Classification: LCC QL758.P37 2016 | DDC 591.5'3--dc23

Published in 2017 by
Gareth Stevens Publishing
111 East 14th Street, Suite 349
New York, NY 10003

Copyright © 2017 Miles Kelly Publishing Ltd

Publishing Director Belinda Gallagher
Creative Director Jo Cowan
Editorial Director Rosie Neave
Senior Editor Claire Philip
Concept Designer Simon Lee
Volume Designer Simon Lee, Rob Hale
Image Manager Liberty Newton
Production Manager Elizabeth Collins
Reprographics Stephan Davis, Thom Allaway
Assets Lorraine King

Acknowlegements:
The publishers would like to thank the following sources for the use of their photographs:
Key: (m) = main (i) = inset
Front cover: (main) Chris Brunskill/ardea.com, (Wild Nature animal globe) ranker/Shutterstock.com
Back cover: (top) Johan Swanepoel/Shutterstock.com, (bottom) Ronnie Howard/Shutterstock.com
Pages 1 Paul Banton/Shutterstock.com
Pages 4–5 (clockwise from bottom left) Pixtal Images/Photolibrary.com, Rolf Nussbaumer/naturepl.com, Stephen Belcher/Minden Pictures/FLPA, Andy Rouse/naturepl.com, Steven J. Kazlowski/Alamy
Grey wolf (m) Laurent Geslin/naturepl.com, (i) Tim Fitzharris/Minden Pictures/FLPA
Rock python (m) Bruce Davidson/naturepl.com, (i) Peter Blackwell/naturepl.com
Killer whale (m) Brandon Cole/naturepl.com, (i) Hiroya Minakuchi/Minden Pictures/FLPA
Tiger (m) Anup Shah/naturepl.com, (i) Tim Fitzharris/Minden Pictures/FLPA
Eagle owl (m) Juniors Bildarchiv/Photolibrary.com, (i) Malcolm Schuyl/FLPA
Barracuda (m) Jeff Rotman/naturepl.com
Red-bellied piranha (m) Pete Oxford/naturepl.com
Nile crocodile (m) Anup Shah/naturepl.com, (i) Vincent Grafhorst/Minden Pictures/FLPA
Huntsman spider (m) Gerry Ellis/Minden Pictures/FLPA, (i) Nick Garbutt/naturepl.com
Polar bear (m) Rob Reijnen/Minden Pictures/FLPA, (i) T.J. Rich/naturepl.com
Golden eagle (m) Malcolm Schuyl/FLPA, (i) Malcolm Schuyl/FLPA
Solifuge (m) Mark Moffett/Minden Pictures/FLPA, (i) Piotr Naskrecki/Minden Pictures/FLPA
Horned frog (m) Pete Oxford/naturepl.com
Eyelash viper (m) David A. Northcott/Corbis
Spotted hyaena (m) Andrew Parkinson/naturepl.com, (i) Hermann Brehm/naturepl.com
Leopard seal (m) Paul Nicklen/Getty Images, (i) Tui De Roy/Minden Pictures/FLPA
Praying mantis (m) Michael & Patricia Fogden/Minden Pictures/FLPA, (i) Preston-Mafham/Premaphotos/naturepl
African wild dog (m) Bruce Davidson/naturepl.com, (i) ImageBroker/Imagebroker/FLPA
Great white shark (m) Doug Perrine/naturepl.com (i) Brandon Cole/naturepl.com
Least weasel (m) Flip De Nooyer/FN/Minden/FLPA

Every effort has been made to acknowledge the source and copyright holder of each picture.
Miles Kelly Publishing apologizes for any unintentional errors or omissions.

All rights reserved. No part of this book may be reproduced in any form without permission from the publisher, except by a reviewer.

Printed in the United States of America

CPSIA compliance information: Batch CS16GS: For further information contact Gareth Stevens, New York, New York at 1-800-542-2595.

CONTENTS

4 LIFE OR DEATH: IN FOR THE KILL

6 PACK POWER
Gray wolf

8 DEATH HUG
Rock python

10 LETHAL LEAPER
Killer whale

12 STEALTH BITER
Tiger

14 DEATHLY WINGS
Eagle owl

16 FATAL FANGS
Barracuda

17 RAZOR TEETH
Red-bellied piranha

18 ON A ROLL
Nile crocodile

20 CREEPY POISONER
Huntsman spider

22 ARCTIC ASSASSIN
Polar bear

24 WINGED BUTCHER
Golden eagle

26 SHADY STALKER
Solifuge

28 BIG MOUTH
Horned frog

29 SUDDEN STRIKE
Eyelash viper

30 BONE CRUNCHERS
Spotted hyena

32 SNEAK ATTACK
Leopard seal

34 FATAL PETAL
Flower mantis

36 TEAM SLAYERS
African wild dog

38 OPEN WIDE!
Great white shark

40 GLOSSARY

FOR MORE INFORMATION

INDEX

LIFE OR DEATH: IN FOR THE KILL

↓ Success! A pygmy owl returns to its nest with a mouse clutched tight in its talons. But that's only one of three or four it needs every night.

Being a hunter might seem an easy life. After a big meal of meaty nourishment, many predators laze around for days, or even weeks. Few other creatures threaten them, because they're so fierce and dangerous.

But that's only part of the story. When prey is scarce, a predator might weaken and starve through lack of food. After much time and effort tracking a target, the quarry (prey) could race off or slip away at any moment.

When it's finally time to go in for the kill, the victim will almost certainly fight back desperately. Predators need all their strength, speed, skills and weaponry to avoid injury and secure their feast.

WHICH ONE?

1 CHOOSE A VICTIM

An old, tired-looking individual, or one suffering from injury? Perhaps an animal that has been weakened through sickness, or a cute but defenseless youngster? Predators show no mercy as they select the easiest option to kill.

↖ The great barracuda cruises the reef edge, its large eyes watching the shoal closely for any sign of weak or injured fish.

→ The great white smashes into its victim from below with such speed and power that it leaps clean out of the water.

5

↖ The tiger's choice is to stay put and hope the prey wanders within range, or charge from cover and sprint for a kill.

READY NOW!

3 THE ATTACK
The key moment: the predator launches its lightning assault. Whether it's a suffocating bite to the throat, a fast strike with poison fangs, or ripping out the prey's guts, it must be fast.

2 GET UP CLOSE

THE APPROACH
Tactics vary from a simple chase that tires out the victim, to a slow, sneaky stalk as the predator creeps up unseen, to waiting in ambush for hours, even days. Then it's all about sudden surprise...

4 THE KILL
After the first grab, a victim might struggle free or counterattack. The predator is ultra-alert, ready to strike again in an instant. Only when the prey gasps its last breath, is it time to relax and begin the big feed.

DEAD SURE

← Some hunters have extra mouths to feed. Parents demonstrate their kill skills for eager offspring, and share the meal too.

As caribou migrate back into the snowy pine forests for winter, hungry wolves snap at their hooves. The pack members watch and wait for an old, young or sick individual to get slightly detached from the herd – and then its fate is sealed. If it attempts to flee, the pack gives chase. Closing in, the wolves race forwards from different directions to bite and then withdraw. The bewildered victim weakens from blood loss, and rapidly the wolves start their long-awaited feast.

PACK POWER

SNARL...

The pack leaders, or alpha pair, take the lion's share of a big kill. They make sure that lesser members know their place.

SPECIAL FEATURES

SCENT: The wolf's exceptionally keen nose picks up and follows scents that could be two or even three days old.

STAMINA: At a steady "dogtrot," a wolf on the trail of prey can keep going for eight hours, gradually wearing down even the fleetest quarry.

STAR FACT
When food is very scarce, wolf packs may combine to increase hunting success, rather than fight over scraps. One group observed in Alaska numbered more than 40!

Gray wolf

Scientific name: *Canis lupus*
Type: Mammal
Lifespan: 8-12 years
Length: Nose to tail-tip 6.5 ft (2 m)
Weight: More than 110 lb (50-plus kg)
Range: All northern lands
Status: Least concern

LET'S GO...

At a moderate pace, a wolf pack can eat up the miles when in pursuit of worthwhile big prey such as deer, wild sheep and goats.

HEARING: Like radar dishes, the wolf's ears swivel around to listen for faint sounds, not only from prey, but also from pack members and neighboring packs.

COOPERATION: Two or three wolves may work together to ambush the biggest victims, such as an elk (moose) or bison (buffalo).

8

Wild-eyed with terror, the victim struggles to escape the rock python's long fangs, stabbed in with devastating speed during its lightning strike. But the snake's muscular coils have begun to sneak around its body, settling into position as they tense like steel cables. With each of the prey's desperate breaths the coils tighten almost unnoticeably, so that the next breath becomes less possible. As air is squeezed away, so is life, and the python begins its long swallow.

DEATH HUG

SQUEEEZE...

A Thomson's gazelle loses its struggle as the rock python increases its grip. The gazelle will suffocate – or perhaps die of a heart attack.

SPECIAL FEATURES

CAMOUFLAGE: Dull greens and browns are ideal for hiding this massive snake among scrubby plants, rocks, soil, undergrowth – even in trees!

HEAT-SENSING PITS: Small hollows or pits, one under each eye, detect heat (infrared rays) coming from warm-blooded prey.

Rock python

Scientific name: *Python sebae*
Type: Reptile
Lifespan: 25-plus years
Length: 20 ft (6 m), sometimes more
Weight: More than 150 lb (70-plus kg)
Range: Africa south of the Sahara
Status: Not enough information

STAR FACT

Several humans have become snacks for rock pythons over the years, usually young children. In 2009 a farmer was attacked by a rock python but used his mobile phone to summon help, and escaped.

GULP...

The python checks each meal's size and shape before working its extending mouth over one end. For the ground squirrel it's headfirst, so that the legs slide in neatly.

MUSCLES: Along the snake's length different blocks of the main body muscles squeeze or compress at different times to keep up overall relentless pressure.

JAWS: With several bones that make up the jaws being loosely connected, and slack jaw joints, the python's mouth can envelop prey wider than its head.

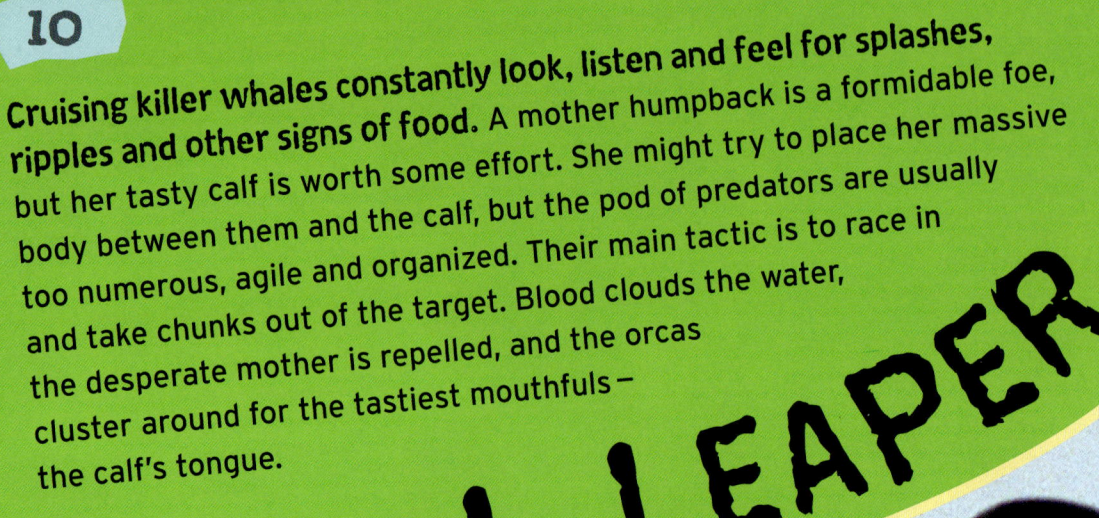

Cruising killer whales constantly look, listen and feel for splashes, ripples and other signs of food. A mother humpback is a formidable foe, but her tasty calf is worth some effort. She might try to place her massive body between them and the calf, but the pod of predators are usually too numerous, agile and organized. Their main tactic is to race in and take chunks out of the target. Blood clouds the water, the desperate mother is repelled, and the orcas cluster around for the tastiest mouthfuls — the calf's tongue.

LETHAL LEAPER

GOTCHA...

A killer whale rides on (and hides within) a breaking wave that takes it onto the beach to within a jaw-snap of a sea lion.

SPECIAL FEATURES

SPEED: A killer whale's super-streamlined body and great strength allow it to cut through open ocean at speeds of more than 37 mph (60 km/h).

AGILITY: Able to turn completely around almost within its own length, the killer whale can also stay mobile underwater for more than 15 minutes.

SPLASH...

Killer whales are among the fastest animals in the sea, so breaching – leaping clear of the water and crashing back in – is easy. Breaching may be a form of communication between pod members.

Killer whale

Scientific name: *Orcinus orca*
Type: Mammal
Lifespan: Up to 60 years, rarely 80-plus
Length: Male up to 29.5 ft (9 m), female 26 ft (8 m)
Weight: Male up to 6.6 tons, female 4.4 tons
Range: All seas and oceans
Status: Not enough information

STAR FACT

Killer whales have huge appetites, eating more than 485 lb (220 kg) of food daily – equivalent to the weight of four average adult humans.

COMMUNICATION: Pod members make varied squeaks and clicks that probably tell each other about food sources or threats such as big sharks.

INTELLIGENCE: Apart from learning many tasks in captivity, wild killer whales regularly devise new ways to hunt prey, such as trapping fish in shallow bays.

A tiger creeps through the long gloomy grass and scrub. It could be dusk, then again, it could be dawn. Tigers prefer to hunt in half-light, but if food is scarce, they will even bear the glare of the midday sun. Tactics depend on the quarry. Generally it's a slow, sneaky stalk to within 55 yards (50 m) of the target, then a massive charge as the big cat bursts from cover, leaps on the prey, and clamps its jaws and teeth onto the victim's neck to choke it to death.

STEALTH BITER

KEEP OUT...

Each tiger patrols and defends its own hunting area (territory), and marks it with droppings, urine and scratched trees. It must ensure enough prey for its own survival and so chases away rival and neighboring tigers — except those of the opposite sex at breeding time.

SPECIAL FEATURES

APPETITE: A large adult tiger can eat almost 66 pounds (30 kg) of food in one session, enough to sustain it for a week or more, but it needs water daily.

SIGHT: Cats' eyes are famously sensitive in the dark. A tiger can see objects more than 109 yards (100 m) away when humans can hardly peer 5.5 yards (5 m).

Tiger

Scientific name: *Panthera tigris*
Type: Mammal
Lifespan: 10–20 years
Length: Head-body up to 8.2 ft (2.5 m), tail up to 3.3 feet (1 m)
Weight: Up to 880 lb (400 kg)
Range: South, East and Southeast Asia
Status: Endangered/Critical

WATCH IT...

A fierce snarl warns others: "Stay away from my prey!" Like all cats, except lions and cheetahs, tigers are solitary predators.

STAR FACT

Each tiger's stripes are as unique as our fingerprints, so human observers can identify individuals. The coloring is also in the skin – shave off a tiger's fur and it would still be striped!

TEETH: The biggest teeth of any carnivore, the tiger's long canines stab and rip flesh. The rows of short incisors between them nibble the flesh from the bone.

SMELL: Tigers find prey such as deer, wild pigs and young buffalo by following scent trails. They also sniff out smaller animals such as lizards and even go fishing.

The woods are quiet as night falls and a young barn owl takes off to hunt mice and voles. Without warning, powerful talons thud into its left side. The hunter becomes the hunted as the great eagle owl, flying noiselessly due to its soft-edged feathers, carries out its mid-air attack. The eagle owl has been scanning with its huge eyes and listening carefully for potential meals – just like the barn owl. Now the latter is mortally wounded and forced to the ground, where its huge relative begins a midnight supper.

DEATHLY WINGS

GLIDE...

Small rodents such as rats, voles, lemmings and mice form the owl's main diet, but a young fox is also welcome.

SPECIAL FEATURES

SIGHT: Most owls can see much the same detail as humans, or better, but in light levels down to 100 times lower, which to us would be pitch black.

SOUND RECEPTION: The owl's "facial disc" of feathers may help to gather sounds, like a radar bowl, and funnel them around to the ears.

LOOK OUT...

An owl's eyes occupy half of its head. Too large to swivel in their sockets, the bird must twist its neck instead – even to look behind itself.

STAR FACT

What look like tufted "horns" or "ears" are actually extra-long feathers on top of the eagle owl's head. The real ears are under the feathers on the sides of the head.

Eagle owl

Scientific name: *Bubo bubo*
Type: Bird
Lifespan: 15-20 years
Length: 29.5 in (75 cm)
Wingspan: 6.6 ft (2 m)
Weight: Male 6.6 lb (3 kg), female up to 8.8 lb (4 kg)
Range: Central Europe across to East Asia
Status: Least concern

HEARING: The eagle owl can locate prey by hearing alone using its amazingly sensitive ears, one offset slightly higher than the other on the head.

TERRITORY DEFENSE: Intruding owls that threaten an eagle owl's territory, which averages 25-31 square miles (40-50 sq km), are flapped at, pecked and scratched.

In deep water, where prey is scarce, it makes sense to ensure your catching technique is as secure as possible. The barracuda's long, fang-like teeth pierce a slippery victim deeply, so that it cannot wriggle and escape. Then with a massive gulp the meal is swallowed into the cavernous gullet. The whole event lasts just three seconds, and the sleek, speedy predator may not eat again for three weeks.

FATAL FANGS

Barracuda

Scientific name: Sphyraena (various species)
Type: Fish
Lifespan: 10-15 years
Length: Up to 5.9 ft (1.8 m)
Weight: Up to 110 lb (50 kg)
Range: Warmer seas and oceans
Status: Not assessed

BACK OFF...

On the edge of the twilight zone, 550 yards (500 m) below the ocean surface, a deep-sea barracuda emerges from the shadows and bares its fangs to ward off threats.

'STAR FACT'

Great barracudas are known to attack human divers, nipping them hard to see if they are tasty enough for a full attack.

SPECIAL FEATURES

SPEED: Barracudas are long, slim and big-tailed, designed for fast acceleration as they burst into action and grab prey with a lightning dash.

SIGHT: The eyes are especially large in deep-water barracuda species, allowing them to see the shadowy shapes of prey in the gloom.

RAZOR TEETH

17

Piranhas can be peaceful, feeding as quiet individuals on worms, water bugs and even fallen fruits. But the slightest scent of blood or body fluids makes a shoal mass together to search for the source. Within seconds of finding it they hurl themselves into a feeding frenzy as they snap and slice with their blade-like teeth. They can become so frantic that they even take chunks out of each other.

Red-bellied piranha

Scientific name: Pygocentrus nattereri
Type: Fish
Lifespan: 10 years
Length: 11.8–15.7 in (30–40 cm)
Weight: 6.6 lb (3 kg)
Range: Central America, North to Central South America
Status: Least concern

SLASH...

The thin, triangular teeth easily cut into skin and tough flesh. The fish clamps its jaws and shakes from side to side to rip off a morsel.

STAR FACT

Stories about piranha shoals stripping all flesh from a large animal such as a cow, leaving only the skeleton, are – true!

SPECIAL FEATURES

SENSES: A stripe along each side of the body, the lateral line, detects ripples so that the piranha can find a struggling animal even in the dark.

SPEED: Using their lateral lines, feeding piranhas sense where other shoal members are, dash in, take a bite and withdraw, all in half a second.

Nile crocodiles wait patiently as thundering hooves, snorts and swirling dust announce that the annual wildebeest trek has reached the river once more. Tumbling and plunging into the water, the 'beests set off in panic to the other side. But hidden menaces approach those swimming along the edge of the main group. Suddenly one wildebeest roars in pain, thrashes wildly – and disappears. A crocodile drags it under until it drowns, then prepares to "death-roll" and rip a haunch from the corpse.

ON A ROLL

STAR FACT

In the "death roll" the croc grabs part of the prey animal's body and then spins like a top to twist and tear a lump of flesh away from the main carcass.

FULL UP... After an enormous meal the Nile crocodile may not need to eat again for four months or more.

SPECIAL FEATURES

SPEED: With a swish of its mighty tail, a croc can accelerate to cover three times its body length in hardly a second.

TEETH: Ongoing replacement and growth happen when a tooth wears and falls out or is damaged. Teeth of different ages give the "ragged smile" look.

OUCH...

Once the jaws clamp onto a victim with a crunching clench, the battle is almost over. The croc can hang on for hours; the wildebeest cannot.

Nile crocodile

Scientific name: *Crocodylus niloticus*
Type: Reptile
Lifespan: 50-plus years
Length: Male up to 18 ft (5.5 m), female 13 ft (4 m)
Weight: Male up to 1,250 lb (570 kg), female 660 lb (300 kg)
Range: Northeast, Central and Southern Africa
Status: Least concern

BITE POWER: The croc's jaw strength and bite pressure have been measured as exceeding those of a great white shark and a lion.

DEFENSE: Crocodile skin is thick and leathery, covered by very hard scales and contains plates of bone within its thickness, for three-layered protection.

With its curiously cramped, crab-like gait, the huntsman spider stalks along a branch in search of a suitable snack. Perhaps a beetle or small lizard, a resting cricket or sleepy moth – even a baby bird in its nest. When the spider detects vibrations that indicate a nearby animal, it swivels around to give its beady eyes a good view. Creeping stealthily into range, it suddenly lunges, grabs with its forelegs, and jabs in venom with its fearsome fangs.

CREEPY POISONER

STAR FACT

Huntsman spiders are also called rain spiders because they seek shelter from storms by hiding in garages, sheds and houses. If you found one in your house, how would you react?

ATTACK...

With its two venomous fangs partly hidden by long hairs, the huntsman is poised to attack, and can subdue a lizard bigger than itself.

SPECIAL FEATURES

SPEED: Huntsman spiders are also called giant crab spiders. Their long, curved, forward-arching legs equip them for sudden sprints.

TOUCH: Hairs on the huntsman's legs are very sensitive to air movements, while its feet detect vibrations caused by animals moving nearby.

Huntsman spider

Scientific name: *Heteropoda*, *Palystes* and others
Type: Arachnid
Lifespan: 15-plus years
Leg span: Up to 11.8 in (30 cm)
Range: Tropical areas including Southeast Asia, Australia, Southern Africa
Status: Not assessed

21

Like other arachnids, insects and crabs, a huntsman grows by shedding its old skin (exoskeleton). The soft new one beneath expands before it hardens.

wow...

VISION: Huntsman spiders do not build webs. Instead their eight main forward-facings eyes give excellent vision for tracking and tackling prey.

POISON: Huntsman venom paralyzes its small victims in seconds. It can cause swelling, nausea and headaches in humans, but death is exceptionally rare.

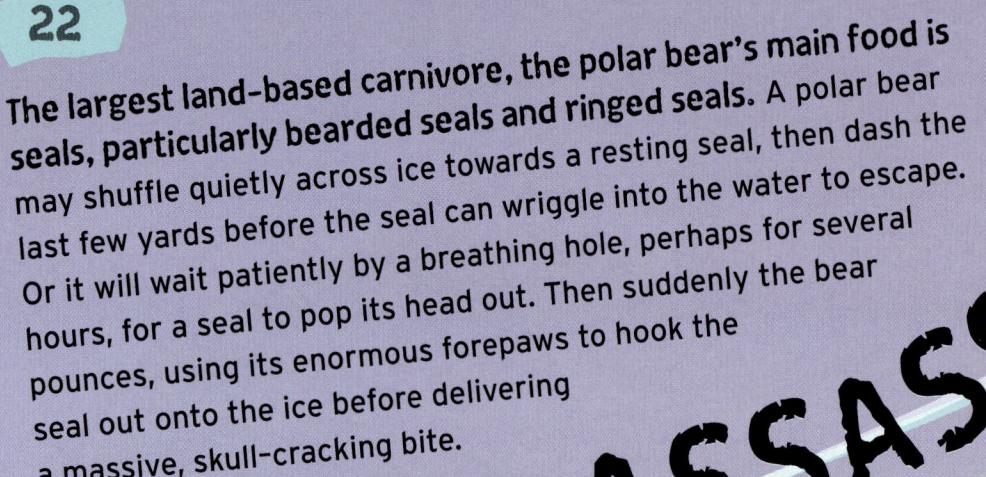

The largest land-based carnivore, the polar bear's main food is seals, particularly bearded seals and ringed seals. A polar bear may shuffle quietly across ice towards a resting seal, then dash the last few yards before the seal can wriggle into the water to escape. Or it will wait patiently by a breathing hole, perhaps for several hours, for a seal to pop its head out. Then suddenly the bear pounces, using its enormous forepaws to hook the seal out onto the ice before delivering a massive, skull-cracking bite.

ARCTIC ASSASSIN

COOL...

Younger polar bears play-fight to practice their killing maneuvers and develop powerful muscles.

SPECIAL FEATURES

FUR: The long hairs of the outer "guard" layer of a polar bear's coat may be more than 4 inches (10 cm) in length. They are not white but transparent.

BLUBBER: Under the bear's skin is a fatty layer of insulating blubber. At the coldest times of year, when prey is scarce, it may be over 4 inches (10 cm) thick.

YUMMY...

A 110-pound (50 kg) seal will be mostly devoured, especially the rich blubber under its skin, which provides the bear with energy, helping it stay warm.

Polar bear

Scientific name: Ursus maritimus
Type: Mammal
Lifespan: 20 years
Length: Male up to 10 ft (3 m), female about 8 ft (2.5 m)
Weight: Male up to 1,320 lb (600 kg), female 660 lb (300 kg)
Range: Far northern lands and seas
Status: Vulnerable

STAR FACT

When lack of sea ice prevents polar bears from catching their usual meaty prey, they may resort to berries, plant buds and even seaweed!

PAWS: The enormous paws, up a foot (30 cm) wide, work as weight-distributing snowshoes on land and as paddles when swimming. The furry soles grip ice well.

SMELL: With the wind in the right direction, and few other scents to interfere, a polar bear can detect a whale or seal carcass from 3 miles (5 km) or more away.

24

The golden eagle can soar on high, spotting prey as small as voles from more than a half mile (1 km) away. Or it may drift low behind trees and suddenly carry out a surprise attack, spearing its talons into a victim such as a rabbit. The eagle's flapping muscles and vast wings have enough power to lift loads that few other flyers could manage. Usually the eagle carries its prize to its eyrie (nest) and tears it apart for its own consumption – or for its offspring.

WINGED BUTCHER

GROSS...

The eagle makes short work of victims by holding them down with its talons and tearing off lumps of the juiciest flesh like an expert butcher, using its sharp-edged, hook-tipped bill.

SPECIAL FEATURES

SIGHT: Large eyes adapted for long-distance vision mean a golden eagle can see details almost ten times farther away than humans can.

FLIGHT: Soaring on updrafts of air among the mountains allows the eagle to circle for hours without a flap, saving energy for that killer swoop.

Golden eagle

Scientific name: *Aquila chrysaetos*
Type: Bird
Lifespan: 30-plus years
Length: over 3 ft (1 m)
Wingspan: about 8 ft (2.4 m)
Weight: about 13 lb (6 kg)
Range: Temperate northern lands
Status: Least concern

STAR FACT

In many areas, rabbits and hares form more than half of the eagle's diet. Larger prey include deer fawns, the young of wild sheep and goats, and in one case, even a bear cub.

SWOOP...

With wing and tail flight feathers fanned to slow its speed, a golden eagle's outstretched talons are ready to impale a meal in their iron grip.

TALONS: Each foot claw is curved almost at a right angle, and on contact the front and rear toes swing together, nearly meeting inside the victim's body.

STRENGTH: It's estimated that a golden eagle can fly while carrying a load of half its own body weight. Larger victims are ripped apart where they died.

Like its cousins, the true spiders, a solifuge or sun spiders is a terrifically efficient eight-legged hunting machine. Also known as the camel spider, sun scorpion or wind scorpion, the solifuge can stalk slowly or sprint with breathtaking speed. Most likely to dash out from a shady crack under a rock and sink its fangs into prey, its food varies from small beetles and worms up to lizards and birds bigger than itself.

SHADY STALKER

STAR FACT

"Solifuge" means "sun hider." Local people have long checked their clothes and footwear before getting dressed, in case a solifuge has sought shade inside.

SPECIAL FEATURES

SIGHT: The solifuge has small eyes on the front part of its main body, which sense little detail but register movement very accurately.

FANGS: The two "fangs" (chelicerae) are hinged to work like pointed, stabbing pincers, and they are moved by extremely powerful muscles.

GNASH...

Long fangs probe for a weak point in the lizard's neck, ready for the mouthparts to scrape up flesh.

Solifuge

Scientific name: *Eremorhax* and others
Type: Arachnid
Lifespan: 10-plus years
Length: Body up to 3.9 in (10 cm)
Leg span: Up to 5.9 in (15 cm)
Range: Much of North America, Africa, Asia
Status: Not assessed

HAIRY...

Sensitive hairs over the legs respond to the slightest vibration. The fangs are mounted on long, fleshy bases but, unlike spiders, lack venom.

PALPS: Two long sensory parts called palps, one on either side of the head just in front of the first true leg, pick up vibrations and help to restrain prey.

LEGS: The first pair of true legs are shorter and specialized for holding victims, while the other six legs are long for exceptionally rapid running.

BIG MOUTH

Almost any creature that can be stuffed into its wide mouth is fair game for the horned frog — even other horned frogs. Mice, lizards, fish, and large insects and worms are also consumed into the sticky, sharp-edged, tough-skinned, gulping jaws. After a full feast this frog — which usually appears to consist of just a mouth, eyes, stomach and four little limbs — looks even more plump and rotund than normal.

Horned frog

Scientific name: Ceratophrys cornuta
Type: Amphibian
Lifespan: 4-6 years
Length: Male 7 in (18 cm), female about 9 in (23 cm)
Weight: Up to 2.2 lb (1 kg)
Range: Northern South America
Status: Least concern

SLURP...

The horned frog may not look speedy, but its sudden lunge from under leaves or within undergrowth is a deadly surprise for most prey.

STAR FACT

Even though its mouth is as wide as its whole head, sometimes a victim is too big and the horned frog may choke to death.

SPECIAL FEATURES

DEFENSE: The leathery skin is difficult for predators to grasp, and the frog also oozes foul liquid, hisses and kicks out in self-defense.

TEETH: Unusually among frogs and toads, the horned frog has small teeth in its upper jaw, which help to subdue kicking, thrashing prey.

SUDDEN STRIKE

Coiled around a branch, the eyelash viper can remain perfectly still for hours. The onset of night brings the best feeding time as the snake use its eyes and the heat-sensitive pit organs just beneath them to assess its surroundings in total darkness. If a mouse or tree rat wanders within range, the snake strikes with lightning speed, delivers its paralyzing venom and begins its meal.

STRIKE...
Poison, quickly injected through the viper's fangs, affects the victim's blood, brain and nerve system.

Eyelash viper
Scientific name: *Bothriechis schlegelii*
Type: Reptile
Lifespan: 8–12 years
Length: 31.5 in (80 cm)
Weight: 4.4 lb (2 kg)
Range: Forests of Central and South America
Status: Not assessed

STAR FACT
The "eyelashes" of this viper are actually angled scales that help with camouflage by breaking up the recognizable outline of the head.

SPECIAL FEATURES

PITS: Small hollows, one between each eye and nostril, detect the heat or infrared rays from warm-blooded prey even in darkness.

FOLDING FANGS: The two long upper front teeth, normally pointing rearwards, fold or tilt down to jab venom into the prey.

BONE CRUNCHERS

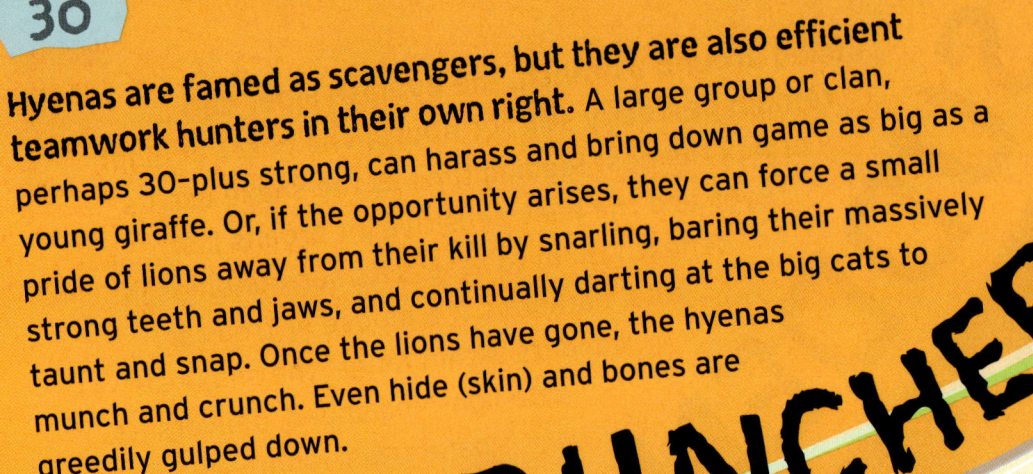

Hyenas are famed as scavengers, but they are also efficient teamwork hunters in their own right. A large group or clan, perhaps 30-plus strong, can harass and bring down game as big as a young giraffe. Or, if the opportunity arises, they can force a small pride of lions away from their kill by snarling, baring their massively strong teeth and jaws, and continually darting at the big cats to taunt and snap. Once the lions have gone, the hyenas munch and crunch. Even hide (skin) and bones are greedily gulped down.

The "laughing" hyena's giggling yelp usually tells other clan members: "Back off, this is my food!"

HA-HA...

SPECIAL FEATURES

JAWS: Massive jaw bones and chewing muscles allow hyenas to crack open bones to get at the nutritious marrow inside.

TEETH: A hyena's teeth are larger than average for its body size, especially the bone-crushing premolars and shearing molars (at front and back).

CHOMP...

There's no time for manners as the hyenas plunge into the carcass innards, consuming first the flesh and guts, then sinew and bone.

Spotted hyena

Scientific name: *Crocuta crocuta*
Type: Mammal
Lifespan: 10-12 years
Length: Male about 5 ft (1.6 m), female up to 6 ft (1.8 m)
Weight: Male about 145 lb (65 kg), female up to 155 lb (70 kg)
Range: Central, East and Southern Africa
Status: Least concern

STAR FACT

Behaviors and body language indicate an individual's rank in the clan. "Crawling" (keeping low to the ground when moving) is a low-ranking hyena's way of showing submission to the boss.

DIGESTION: Extra-strong digestive acids and juices make short work of swallowed bony bits, dissolving them to extract as much goodness as possible.

STRENGTH: Hyenas' powerful shoulders and front legs, used for tearing prey and self-defense, contrast with their sloping backs and smaller rumps and rear legs.

Penguins beware! The leopard seal sometimes strikes from below, rising from the deep with the tiniest swish to sink its teeth into the bird's chest fat and flesh. Or this long, slim, sneaky speedster may lie in wait under the edge of an iceberg, then dash out as a penguin dives in, so fast that the unlucky victim plunges headfirst into its jaws. When penguins are too scared to swim, the leopard seal switches to fish, squid, or perhaps a smaller seal such as the crabeater.

SNEAK ATTACK

Terrified penguins huddle on a mound in the center of an ice floe as a leopard seal patrols the surrounding waters.

BEWARE

Leopard seal

Scientific name: *Hydrurga leptonyx*
Type: Mammal
Lifespan: 22-28 years
Length: Male 11.2 ft (3.4 m), female up to 12.3 ft (3.8 m)
Weight: Male 880 lb (400 kg), female up to 1,100 lb (500 kg)
Range: Southern Ocean, Antarctica
Status: Least concern

SPECIAL FEATURES

SWIMMING: Cruising with hardly a ripple, the seal accelerates to full speed in a split second, and twists and turns after the most agile prey.

BREATHING: Holding its breath for more than 30 minutes means the leopard seal can surprise penguins that thought it was long gone.

STAR FACT

The first recorded human death from a leopard seal happened in 2003, when a snorkeling research scientist was dragged under and drowned.

YIKES...

If a swimming penguin gets this close to a leopard seal, it's staring death in the face. With only one-tenth of a second to react, it's probably already too late.

SENSES AND STRENGTH: This seal can see a resting penguin or seal through thin ice from below, swim up and smash through, right in front of the victim.

TEETH: The 1.2-inch (3 cm) long, doglike canine teeth are ideal to jab into the prey as the seal shakes the life out of it and rips it into smaller chunks that it can swallow.

A butterfly flutters down to sip nectar from a beautiful flower, unaware that among the petals sits death in disguise – a spiny flower mantis. Its eyes swivel to check the butterfly's distance, then in a flash, the jackknife front legs shoot fowards and snap together to impale the victim with their strong spines. The mantis settles down to chew off the butterfly's head, then nibbles its way along the body. Eating the wings too means it's really hungry.

FATAL PETAL

STAR FACT

This insect's bent front limbs give it the common name "praying" mantis, as though its hands are together in worship – but it is far more efficient at "preying."

TRAPPED...

The jointed front legs work like spiked scissors that flick shut powerfully and instantly.

SPECIAL FEATURES

SIGHT: The huge eyes of the mantis are almost as large as the rest of the head and see not only great detail but also very fast movements.

FORELEGS: The fierce thornlike spines on the front legs stab deep into prey so that it cannot struggle free.

Flower mantis

Scientific name: *Pseudocreobotra* and others (various species)
Type: Insect
Lifespan: 5 years
Length: 1.6–2 in (4–5 cm)
Wingspan: 2.4 in (6 cm)
Range: East and Southern Africa
Status: Not assessed

Keeping very still while on view is key to the mantis' hunting success. "Petals" that move will scare away visitors at once.

FREEZE...

CAMOUFLAGE: Each flower mantis has a unique pattern of colors and shapes, mainly pinks and greens, and selects a flower of the same hues in which to lurk.

MOUTHPARTS: The mantis has two sharp-edged mandibles that move sideways (not up and down), coming together in the center like powerful pincers.

Dogged pursuit is the speciality of African wild dogs. Once a pack latches onto the scent of an antelope or similar quarry, they can run for hours… and hours… The prey is finally exhausted and panting when the dogs rush in for a massed attack. Snapping and scratching, the pack's lead hunters grab the animal's nose and rear unprotected underbelly. Within seconds, the dogs start to gorge their fill. Within a minute, death is merciful.

TEAM SLAYERS

STAR FACT

The African wild dog is a champion eater. It can gulp down more than 22 pounds (10 kg) — about one-third of its own weight — of muscle, sinew, chewed skin and crushed bone.

NO ESCAPE…

Even if the wind blows the scent of prey animals away from the wild dog's ultra-sensitive nose, its rounded ears will pick up distant munching sounds, hoof-falls and snorts.

SPECIAL FEATURES

APPETITE: The wild dogs' legendary stomach capacity means they consume a carcass before hungry lions or scavenging hyenas muscle in.

STAMINA: With their long legs and lean build, wild dogs are relatively lightweight but still well muscled. They easily trot more than 12 miles (20 km) during a hunt.

African wild dog

Scientific name: *Lycaon pictus*
Type: Mammal
Lifespan: 12–18 years
Shoulder height: 29.5 in (75 cm)
Length: Head-body about 35 in (90 cm), tail about 14 in (35 cm)
Weight: 55–66 lb (25–30 kg)
Range: East and Southern Africa
Status: Endangered

DOOMED...

A wildebeest struggles in vain under the combined teeth and pulling power of a wild dog pack. A dozen or more dogs cluster around, subdue the animal and start to feed.

COMMUNICATION: Pack individuals keep in contact with strange, birdlike cheeps, twitters and mini-yelps to coordinate the hunt's progress and tactics.

TEAMWORK: "Outrider" and "pursuer" dogs guide the victim towards the bigger, stronger members that lead the final assault.

Triangular fins cut the water's surface, but the swimming seal is not yet in mortal danger. It can usually cope with two or three great whites, being able to twist and dash away as they approach. It's not far now to the beach… BANG… an unseen great white surges up from below and slams its teeth into the seal's chest. A ferocious bite, a fatal injury, and the seal thrashes in a cloud of its own blood. The sharks wait a few more seconds for the dying creature to weaken before closing in.

OPEN WIDE!

SMILE…

The upper teeth are triangular with serrated edges, while the lower ones are more pointed and smooth-edged, like small daggers.

SPECIAL FEATURES

TEETH: More than 50 teeth are in use at the front of the mouth. Behind these are several more rows ready to come into action as older teeth break off.

JAWS: The legendary jaw muscles and bite power of the great white are greater than most other creatures, including wolves.

STAR FACT

A large great white can swallow more than 33 pounds (15 kg) in one gulp, which is equivalent to the weight of a three-year-old human child.

Great white shark

Scientific name: Carcharodon carcharias
Type: Fish
Lifespan: 20-30 years, rarely 50-plus
Length: 20, maybe 23 ft (6-7 m) (females usually larger)
Weight: Up to 2.2 tons
Range: All warm and temperate seas
Status: Endangered

WARMING UP...

The great white is partly warm-blooded, able to raise its brain and muscle temperatures to 50°F (10°C) above its surroundings.

SMELL: The nostril pits can scent the tiniest amounts of blood and other body fluids spreading through the water from hundreds of yards away.

ELECTRO-SENSE: Tiny hole-like pits, "ampullae of Lorenzini," dotted over the snout detect faint electrical pulses from the active muscles of other creatures.

GLOSSARY

ambush a surprise attack assassin; someone or something that kills with a sudden attack
captivity the state of being caged
carnivore an animal that eats meat
exoskeleton the hard outer covering of an animal's body
prey an animal that is hunted by other animals for food
scavenger an animal that eats the remains of dead animals
stealth the act of doing something quietly and secretly
territory an area of land that an animal considers to be its own and will fight to defend
venom something an animal makes in its body that can harm other animals

FOR MORE INFORMATION

BOOKS

Graham, Anna. *Top 10s: Fierce Predators*. New York, NY: Bearport Publishing, 2005.
Taylor, Barbara. *3-D Explorer: Predators*. San Diego, CA: Silver Dolphin Books, 2014.

WEBSITES

Nat Geo Wild: Deadly 60
http://animals.nationalgeographic.com/animals/wild/shows-deadly-60/pictures/
Learn about and see photos of many fierce predators.

Predation
http://www.kidzsearch.com/wiki/Predation
Read more about predators and their prey.

INDEX

ambush 5, 7
camouflage 8, 29, 35
carnivore 13, 22
communication 11, 37
ears 7, 14, 15, 36
eyes 4, 8, 12, 14, 15, 16, 20, 21, 24, 26, 28, 29, 34

fangs 5, 8, 16, 17, 20, 26, 27, 29
humans 9, 11, 12, 13, 14, 21, 24, 33, 39
jaw 9, 10, 12, 17, 19, 28, 30, 32, 38
muscle 9, 22, 24, 26, 30, 36, 38, 39

speed 4, 5, 8, 10, 16, 17, 20, 25, 26, 28, 29, 32
talons 4, 14, 24, 25
teeth 12, 13, 16, 17, 18, 28, 29, 30, 32, 33, 37, 38
territory 12, 15
venom 20, 21, 27, 29

Publisher's note to educators and parents: Our editors have carefully reviewed these websites to ensure that they are suitable for students. Many websites change frequently, however, and we cannot guarantee that a site's future contents will continue to meet our high standards of quality and educational value. Be advised that students should be closely supervised whenever they access the Internet.